BABIES

Sandy Caporale

Rigby®

A Harcourt Achieve Imprint

www.Rigby.com
1-800-531-5015

Babies need many things.
This baby needs to eat.

Babies need many things.
This baby needs to drink.

Babies need many things. This baby needs to play.

Babies need many things.
This baby needs to smile.

Babies need many things.
This baby needs to cry.

Babies need many things.
This baby needs to hug.

Babies need many things.
This baby needs to rock.

Babies need many things.
This baby needs to sleep.